Measuring Time

Seasons of the Year

Tracey Steffora

Heinemann Library
Chicago, Illinois

www.heinemannraintree.com
Visit our website to find out more information about Heinemann-Raintree books.

To order:

☎ Phone 888-454-2279

💻 Visit www.heinemannraintree.com to browse our catalog and order online.

© 2011 Heinemann Library
an imprint of Capstone Global Library, LLC
Chicago, Illinois

Edited by Tracey Steffora and Dan Nunn
Designed by Richard Parker
Picture research by Hannah Taylor
Originated by Capstone Global Library Ltd
Printed in China

14 13 12 11
10 9 8 7 6 5 4 3 2 1

ISBN 978-1-4329-5788-9 (saddle-stitch)

Library of Congress Cataloging-in-Publication Data
Cataloging-in-Publication data is available at the Library of Congress.

006125/042011

Acknowledgments
We would like to thank the following for permission to reproduce photographs: Alamy Images pp. **4** (©Cultura), **15** (©RubberBall), **22 top right** (©Jon Helgason); Corbis pp. **5** (epa/Kay Nietfeld), **21** (Blend Images/Jamie Grill/JGI); istockphoto pp. **6** (©Ermin Gultenberger), **14** (©LeoGrand), **16** (©Primary Picture), **19** (©Morley Read), **22 bot** (©mammamaart), **22 top left** (©David Safanda); NASA p. **23 top**; Photolibrary pp. **10** (Comstock), **18** (Superstock); shutterstock pp. **7** (©Kai Schirmer), **8** (©Foto Yakov), **11** (©Nagel Photography), **12** (©RazvanZinica), **13** (©Shebeko), **17** (©Dennis Donohue), **20** (©Graeme Dawes), **23 bot** (oriontrail).

Front cover photographs of sunflowers reproduced with permission of Alamy Images (©David Norton Photograghy), autumn leaves reproduced with permission of Alamy Images (©Bob Handelman), frosted pine needles reproduced with permission of Alamy Images (©Christina Bollen) and tree bud reproduced with permission of Photolibrary (Mixa). Back cover photograph of a person sliding down a snowy hill reproduced with permission of istockphoto (© Ermin Gultenberger).

Every effort has been made to contact copyright holders of any material reproduced in this book. Any omissions will be rectified in subsequent printings if notice is given to the publisher.

Contents

Time and Seasons

Time is how long something takes.

Time is when things happen.

Some things take a short time.

Some things take a long time.

A season is a long amount of time.

There are four seasons in one year.

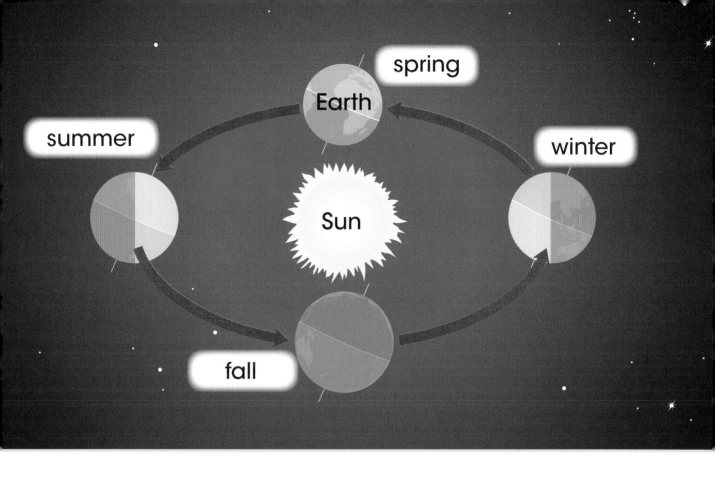

The seasons change as the Earth travels around the Sun.

Winter

In winter we feel the cold.

In winter we taste hot chocolate.

In winter we hear the wind.

In winter we see bare trees.

Spring

In spring we feel warm weather.

In spring we hear birds sing.

In spring we see new plants.

In spring we smell flowers.

Summer

In summer we feel the heat.

In summer we see the bright Sun.

In summer we taste fresh berries.
In summer we hear water splash.

Fall

In fall we feel cool air.

In fall we hear leaves crunch.

In fall we feel a warm sweater.

In fall we see birds flying south.

In fall we see leaves change color.

Around the World

Some places are always cold.

Some places are always hot.

January						
Mo	Tu	We	Th	Fr	Sa	Su
01	02	03	04	05	06	07
08	09	10	11	12	13	14
15	16	17	18	19	20	21
22	23	24	25	26	27	28
29	30	31				

February						
Mo	Tu	We	Th	Fr	Sa	Su
			01	02	03	04
05	06	07	08	09	10	11
12	13	14	15	16	17	18
19	20	21	22	23	24	25
26	27	28				

March						
Mo	Tu	We	Th	Fr	Sa	Su
			01	02	03	04
05	06	07	08	09	10	11
12	13	14	15	16	17	18
19	20	21	22	23	24	25
26	27	28	29	30	31	

April						
Mo	Tu	We	Th	Fr	Sa	Su
30						01
02	03	04	05	06	07	08
09	10	11	12	13	14	15
16	17	18	19	20	21	22
23	24	25	26	27	28	29

May						
Mo	Tu	We	Th	Fr	Sa	Su
01	02	03	04	05	06	
07	08	09	10	11	12	13
14	15	16	17	18	19	20
21	22	23	24	25	26	27
28	29	30	31			

June						
Mo	Tu	We	Th	Fr	Sa	Su
			01	02	03	
04	05	06	07	08	09	10
11	12	13	14	15	16	17
18	19	20	21	22	23	24
25	26	27	28	29	30	

July						
Mo	Tu	We	Th	Fr	Sa	Su
30	31					01
02	03	04	05	06	07	08
09	10	11	12	13	14	15
16	17	18	19	20	21	22
23	24	25	26	27	28	29

August						
Mo	Tu	We	Th	Fr	Sa	Su
01	02	03	04	05		
06	07	08	09	10	11	12
13	14	15	16	17	18	19
20	21	22	23	24	25	26
27	28	29	30	31		

September						
Mo	Tu	We	Th	Fr	Sa	Su
				01	02	
03	04	05	06	07	08	09
10	11	12	13	14	15	16
17	18	19	20	21	22	23
24	25	26	27	28	29	30

October						
Mo	Tu	We	Th	Fr	Sa	Su
01	02	03	04	05	06	07
08	09	10	11	12	13	14
15	16	17	18	19	20	21
22	23	24	25	26	27	28
29	30	31				

November						
Mo	Tu	We	Th	Fr	Sa	Su
		01	02	03	04	
05	06	07	08	09	10	11
12	13	14	15	16	17	18
19	20	21	22	23	24	25
26	27	28	29	30		

December						
Mo	Tu	We	Th	Fr	Sa	Su
31					01	02
03	04	05	06	07	08	09
10	11	12	13	14	15	16
17	18	19	20	21	22	23
24	25	26	27	28	29	30

We use a calendar to know the season.

see   hear   feel   taste   smell

We use our senses to know the season.

What are the seasons like where you live?

Picture Glossary

Earth the planet on which we live

Sun the star that gives heat and light to the Earth; the Earth travels around the Sun

Index

Note to Parents and Teachers

Before reading

Discuss the current season and characteristics of that season where you live. Prompt children to think about the different clothing they might wear during different seasons. Review the five senses with children and begin a discussion of things that they see, hear, smell, feel, and taste each season.

After reading

- Collect photos that illustrate different seasons and use as a sorting activity.
- You might explain to children that a season also refers to a certain time of year that is characterized by a particular event or activity (e.g., strawberry season, football season, allergy season). Encourage them to name and identify other seasons with which they are familiar.

Seasons of the Year

Can you tell what season it is?

Read this book to find out about winter, spring, summer, and fall.

Books in this series introduce children to the concept of time and how we measure time in our daily lives. Each book uses engaging images and simple, repetitive text to make the content accessible for young readers. In **Seasons of the Year**, children are taken on a sensory journey as they learn about how we measure time throughout the seasons.

Titles in the **Measuring Time** series:
Clocks and Calendars
Days of the Week
Hours, Minutes, and Seconds
Months of the Year
Seasons of the Year
Times of the Day

Author
Tracey Steffora, M.Ed., is a writer, artist, and early childhood educator.

Literacy consultant
Nancy E. Harris has her Masters of Education in Reading. She works with children through classroom demonstrations and coaching.

Primary Math

ISBN 978-1-4329-5788-9

9 781432 957889   90000

Acorn books engage early readers in content area learning.

heinemannraintree.com

Level H   Word Count: 180